Change Management

By Sebastian Meyer

Digital Edition

Table of Contents

I. Introduction

Gordon Evans Health and safety change

Taken from: Smith, Peter *''Organisational Behaviour (People and Organisations)''*, revised July 2007, Bristol, UK.

In September 1983 Gordon Evan was promoted to the position of Supervisor, a first line management position in his company. The company was a major British Pharmaceutical company and Gordon Evans group worked on his production on insulin that involved some hazardous substances. Gordon became concerned that his men were not conforming to the agreed health and safety rules for their protection and were running unnecessary risks.

His first action was to remind his group of the need to take precautions when handling hazardous substances. This involved the use of visors to protect their eyes. At first, they improved but then relapsed to their old bad habits. Gordon realised that, as things were it would be a constant struggle to get his men to observe the safety rules. He reasoned that convenience was a major problem. The visors were kept in a cupboard some distance from where the men handled the hazardous liquids.

Hen they did use them, because there were no storage facilities where they were used, the visors quickly became dirty, damaged and unusable. Gordon decided to overcome the 'inconvenience' problem.

In early October he called in the maintenance carpenter Wally Green to see if he could offer any help. Maintenance was not known for being very co-operative, but Gordon decided to give them a try. He explained the problem to Wally and asked him if he had any ideas. To his surprise Wally responded with interest. He suggested making small wooden cupboards with plastic flaps to hold up to three visors. These could be placed either on machine mountings or an adjacent wall, in the place that they were needed. Wally's enthusiasm was explained by the motivation of an innovative idea that would be useful. Normally he carried out routine repairs that soon needed repetition.

Wally had a proto-type ready within a week. Gordon then went to find John Burns who was the work group's health and safety representative. He needed the support of John to sell the new idea to the men. John was enthusiastic about the new idea and made some useful suggestions about where the boxes should be sited. Within a few days Gordon, Wally and John were busy looking at the workstations and deciding where to put the boxes. Their activity aroused the curiosity of the workforce. By the end of the month all the boxes containing new visors were in place and the work group had been briefed. He had no further difficulties with this particular issue. At the November meeting of the supervisors' group Gordon explained his innovation to his fellow managers and the idea was adopted company wide.

II. Main Part

The following report briefly informs through the lenses of relevant theories what kind of ''change models' including change agent skills Gordon has put on show. Having provided you a sharp and well focused analysis of his methods of change management, we comment further on his job competencies[1]. The conclusion is devoted to our final recommendation for Gordon's future.

---

[1] To have an updated idea of new competency models, please read:

Caldwell, R. (2008). *Human Resource Management Journal,* Vol 18, no 3, 275 – 294. London.

Gordon has been employed as a first line supervisor in a major British Pharmaceutical company for 25 years. He has been responsible for his co-workers to carefully respect and throughout maintain the necessary safety as well as health rules. It is one of his most essential core tasks as his group has mainly dealt with chemical materials causing both perilous and serious health hazards. Within a fairly short period of time, he was not only able to get his team to make a consistent prevention by *always* wearing their pair of safety goggles shielding them from hazardous substances. In fact, he has also efficiently realised a crucial company wide safety and health change.

2.1

Gordon's incentive to change is a result of some type of frustration and/ or dissatisfaction that resulted from his group members' resistance to change. This phenomenon clearly devitalises his expectations as a supervisor manager. His discontentedness soon initiates a change process and pushing which somehow induces him to ''*unfreeze*'' (Lewin, 1947) the restraining spirit of his group (which still heads for the ''old bad habits'').

According to Havelock's problem solving model, he initially looks for the ''disturbance of the status quo'' (Havelock, 1969). Gordon has to change in order to meet his personal and managerial *needs*. Although his methods of change management may have reflected the feeling of loss of identity, face and effectiveness, he has yet become motivated to changes in our case study. Moreover, he is capable of balancing the number of threat using his ''survival anxiety'' (Schirm, 1995) by strongly emphasizing his *need* for innovation: First of all, as far as his key tasks are concerned, he is in charge of his team's health and safety at work. Then, concerning his strategic objectives, he aims for shifting and developing a ''new behaviour'' using an innovated approach within his team.

Throughout the actual *''change''* process, Gordon's change agent skills are evident. To change, he explicitly describes and explains Wally Green, a maintenance carpenter, the recent situation and obstacles provoking the ongoing difficulties. In this case, it belongs to his unique and necessary features as a change agent to make use of the initiative even though Wally may not have seemed cooperative in the past. (Lippit, Watson & Westley, 1958).

Indeed, Gordon does not only have a positive influence on Wally's reaction but he also succeeds in encouraging and motivating him for *his* and finally the company's realistic and sustainable innovation. To sum up, Havelock's social interaction model is valid in our case. Gordon successfully asks John Burns to accept *his* innovation since he, who represents the team's safety and health manager, is the ''influential receiver''. After his innovation process has positively come shining through, he ''*refreezes*'' his new idea by describing it to his fellow managers for setting up this new plan company wide. Consequently, he permanently observes it to avoid the ''everything is changing, but nothing holds'' dilemma.

2.2

The second part is regarded as a confidential personal profile report that focuses upon Gordon's profession skills using the ''Spencer General Model'' (Spencer & Spencer, 1995).

One of the most obvious job competencies Gordon puts on show, is *analytical thinking* (Table 1). We derived his ''thinking and solving problem'' capability from his logical problem solving and systematic attitude. He has correctly identified and assessed the ''ongoing problem'' by critically observing the ''inconvenience'' factor in his group. For economically managing this delicate matter, he cleverly combines two influential change models by Havelock (1969) and Lewin (1947). These concepts help him taking the first steps to accomplish his objective.

Furthermore, it is Gordon's way of behaving and ultimately characteristic mentality that *flexibility* (Table 2) is without reservations a precious part of his personal skill portfolio.

Without any doubts, he is an expert at rapidly analyzing as well as clarifying complex problems yet, in essence, he effectively responds to short changes in human behaviour.

He is a unique ''emotion tamer'' who adjusts to the recent atmosphere within his team.

Next, his second strength belongs to the *impact and influence* (Table 3) category. It is just enviable and amazing how his charisma deeply and strongly convinces a ''hard core denier'' within a fairly short period of time. Is a certain number of agreeable sympathy and perseverance of need? We say yes and he has unconsciously kept his ''survival anxiety'' in mind. His colleagues eventually cooperate with him. This feeling immediately backs up his personal and managerial ''needs''. His third eye-catching competency of change management is *relationship building* (Table 4).

We appreciate his well-selected and thorough ''Mafia-making'' strategy as he has actively set up an interpersonal network with one of the most influential manager. Hence, the social interaction model perfectly works and Gordon's idea becomes reality in the company. As a change agent, he has chosen the right strategic partner he achieves his *final goal* with for carrying through his new idea company wide.

We have found Gordon's work outstanding and excellent. For change to happen, people should show readiness (Crego & Schittrin, 1995) for moving towards the new behaviour. In this case study, it is not Gordon's team which is willing to change as it is naturally supposed to, however Gordon himself ultimately gets motivated for the sudden change process and its favourable realization. His traits of character are to be highlighted: He has got a realistic and clear forecast in his mind right from the very beginning of the scenario.

Interestingly, he has immediately recognized that his ''new behaviour'', which aims for innovation, should be someway similar to the ''old behaviour'', which has stressed the team's ''old bad habit''. Alternatively, it could be likely ''forgotten'' or even regarded as a high-turnover like his first attempt. By doing so, he *''refreezes''* his new idea by motivating his team to implicitly hold the ''old tradition''. In summary, he has discovered his ''magic formula'' in (in-)convenience of his team members. Thanks to his self-confidence, tolerance of inner frustration and persistence in the pursuit of realistic goals as well as his charisma, he has quickly mastered a quite challenging objective. No one may deny that his driving force includes *analytical thinking, impact and influence, flexibility and relationship building.* To conclude, our report on Gordon wants to shortly show his techniques of changing.

All in all, we strongly recommend Gordon's innovation be introduced in our company and he be employed on a permanent basis.

III. Appendix

Table 1: Spencer, L.M. & Spencer, S.M. (1995). *Competence at work:* 69.

Table 8–1 Analytical Thinking (AT) Scale

Behavioral Description

COMPLEXITY OF ANALYSIS

- *Not Applicable or None.* Does each thing as it comes up, responds to immediate needs or requests; or work is organized by someone else.
- *Breaks Down Problems.* Breaks problems into simple lists of tasks or activities.
- *Sees Basic Relationships.* Analyzes relationships among a few parts of a problem or situation. Makes simple causal links (A causes B) or pro-and-con decisions. Sets priorities for tasks in order of importance.
- *Sees Multiple Relationships.* Analyzes relationships among several parts of a problem or situation. Breaks down a complex task into manageable parts in a systematic way. Recognizes several likely causes of events, or several consequences of actions. Generally anticipates obstacles and thinks ahead about next steps.
- *Makes Complex Plans or Analyses.* Systematically breaks down a complex problem or process into component parts. Uses several techniques to break apart complex problems to reach a solution; or makes long chains of causal connections.
- *Makes Very Complex Plans or Analyses.* Systematically breaks multidimensional problems or processes into component parts; or uses several analytical techniques to identify several solutions and weighs the value of each.
- *Makes Extremely Complex Plans or Analyses.* Organizes, sequences, and analyzes extremely complex interdependent systems.

SIZE OF PROBLEM ADDRESSED*

- *Concerns One or Two People's Performances.*
- *Concerns a Small Work Unit.* Or concerns a moderate-size sale, or one aspect of a larger unit's performance.
- *Concerns an Ongoing Problem.* May involve a moderate-size work unit, several sales, or a very large sale.
- *Concerns Overall Performance.* Involves performance of a major division of a large company or of an entire small-size company.
- *Concerns Long-Term Performance.* Relates to a major division or entire company in a complex environment (economic or demographic changes, major improvements, etc.).

*Although this scale is strongly related to job size, it is also important in considering placement, since too large a jump in problem size may overload a person's analytic or conceptual capacity.

Table 2: Spencer et al (1995):85.

Table 9-3 Flexibility (FLX) Scale

Behavioral Description

BREADTH OF CHANGE

Counterproductively Sticks to Own Opinion/Tactics/Approach. Despite obvious problems, retains same point of view; does not recognize others' views as valid.

Always Follows Procedures.

Sees Situation Objectively. Recognizes the validity of others' viewpoints.

Flexibly Applies Rules or Procedures. Depending on the individual situation, adapts actions to accomplish organization's larger objectives. Pinch-hits by doing co-workers' tasks as necessary during an emergency.

Adapts Tactics to Situation or to Other's Response. Changes own behavior or approach to suit the situation.

Adapts Own Strategies, Goals, or Projects to Situations.

Makes Organizational Adaptations. Makes smaller or short-term adaptations in own or client company in response to the needs of the situation.

Adapts Strategies. Makes large or long-term adaptations in own or client company in response to the needs of the situation. (This level implies various Influence competencies, and possibly Managerial, Cognitive, or Achievement Competencies.)

SPEED OF ACTION

Long-Term, Considered, or Planned Changes (over a month).

Short-Term Plan to Change (1 week–1 month).

Fast Change (less than a week). This is the default score if the example has an unclear time frame.

Quick Changes (within a day).

Instantaneous Action or Decision to Act. "Turns on a dime."

Table 3: Spencer et al (1995): 46.

Table 6-1 Impact and Influence (IMP) Scale

Level	Behavioral Description

A. ACTIONS TAKEN TO INFLUENCE OTHERS

A. −1 *Personalized Power.* Cutthroat competition within the organization, concern for personal position regardless of organizational damage.

A. 0 *Not Applicable.* Or shows no attempt to influence or persuade others.

A. 1 *States Intention but Takes No Specific Action.* Intends to have a specific effect or impact; expresses concern with reputation, status, and appearance.

A. 2 *Takes a Single Action to Persuade.* Makes no apparent attempt to adapt to the audience's level and interests. Uses direct persuasion in a discussion or presentation (e.g., appeals to reason, data, larger purpose; uses concrete examples, visual aids, demonstrations, etc.).

A. 3 *Takes a Two-Step Action to Persuade.* Makes no apparent adaptation to the level and interests of the audience. Includes careful preparation of data form presentation or the making of two or more different arguments of points in a presentation or a discussion.

A. 4 *Calculates the Impact of One's Action or Words.* Adapts a presentation or discussion to appeal to the interest and level of others. Anticipates the effect of an action or other detail on people's image of the speaker.

A. 5 *Calculates a Dramatic Action.* Models behavior desired in others or takes a well thought-out unusual or dramatic action in order to have a specific impact. [Scoring Note: Threats or displays of anger do not count as dramatic actions to influence: see Directiveness level A-8].

A. 6 *Takes Two Steps to Influence.* With each step adapted to the specific audience or planned to have a specific effect or anticipates and prepares for other's reactions.

A. 7 *Three Actions or Indirect Influence.* Uses experts or other third parties to influence; or takes three different actions or makes complex, staged arguments. Assembles political coalitions, builds "behind-the-scenes" support for ideas, deliberately gives or withholds information in order to have specific effects, uses "group process skills" to lead or direct a group.

A. 8 *Complex Influence Strategies.* Uses complex influence strategies tailored to individual situations (e.g., using chains of indirect influence—"get A to show B so B will tell C such-and-such"), structuring situations or jobs or changing organizational structure to encourage desired behavior; uses complex political maneuvering to reach a goal or have an effect. [This level of complexity of action is usually associated with levels 4, 5, and 6 of Interpersonal Understanding, or with corresponding levels of Organizational Awareness.]

B. BREADTH OF INFLUENCE, UNDERSTANDING, OR NETWORK (Own or Other Organization)

B. 1 *One Other Person.*

B. 2 *Work Unit or Project Team.*

B. 3 *Department.*

Table 4: Spencer et al (1995):52.

Table 6–3 Relationship Building (RB) Scale*

Level	Behavioral Description
A.	CLOSENESS OF RELATIONSHIPS BUILT
A. 0	*Avoids Contact.* Reclusive, avoids social interactions.
A. 1	*Accepts Invitations.* Accepts invitations or other friendly overtures from others, but does not extend invitations or go out of the way to establish working relationships.
A. 2	*Makes Work-Related Contacts.* Maintains formal working relationships (largely confined to work-related matters, not necessarily formal in tone or style or structure). Includes unstructured chats about work-related matters.
A. 3	*Makes Occasional Informal Contact.* Occasionally initiates informal or casual relationships at work, chats about children, sports, news, etc.
A. 4	*Builds Rapport.* Frequently initiates informal or casual contacts at work with associates or customers. Makes a conscious effort to build rapport.
A. 5	*Makes Occasional Social Contacts.* Occasionally initiates or pursues friendly relationships with associates or customers outside work at clubs, restaurants, etc.
A. 6	*Makes Frequent Social Contacts.* Frequently initiates or pursues friendly relationships with associates or customers outside work at clubs, restaurants, etc.
A. 7	*Makes Home and Family Contacts.* Occasionally brings associates or customers home or goes to their home.
A. 8	*Makes Close Personal Friendships.* Frequently entertains associates or customers at home. Becomes close personal friends with them; or utilizes personal friendships to expand business network.

VI. References

Crego, E.T. & Schittrn, P.D. (1995). *Customer – centered reengineering Remapping for total customer value.* New York: Irwin, Burr Ridge.

Havelock, R.G. (1969). *Planning for innovation through Dissemination and Utilization of Knowledge.* Michigan: Ann Arbor: Institute for Social Research.

Lewin, K. (1947). *Field Theory in Social Science.* New York: Harper Row.

Lippit, Watson & Westley (1958). *Dynamics of planned change.* New York: Harcourt & Brace.

Schirm, E.H. (1995). *Kurt Lewin's change theory in the field and in the classroom: Note towards a model of managed learning.* Massachusetts: Susan Whulan: Cambridge.

Spencer, L.M. & Spencer S.M. (1995). *Competence at work.* New York: John Wiley.